In 2009 I was on an intense quest of true worship and communion with God. While on this journey, my sister-in-love asked me about hearing God's voice. I explained it to her the best way I could.

I began thinking how to hear God is an extremely common question amongst His people and I wanted to explain it better.

I sought the Lord day and night about how to convey a universal lesson for the people to learn how to hear His voice. The Lord gave me Psalm 100.

After the Lord showed me the connection with hearing Him and Psalm 100, the Holy Spirit inspired me to write an essay on *Hearing the Voice of God*. Later I spoke on the subject at a Father's Day Breakfast and then taught a series on it for a Young-Adult Bible Group. During the series, this devotional was created.

Now, I am humbly honored to have this devotional made available for you.

<u>Dedication</u>

After completing this devotional and doing the final edits, I realized there was no dedication. I said to myself, who can I dedicate this to... help Lord? The Spirit said to me, what are your experiences with Psalm 100?

I began to think immediately of going to church as a child and every Sunday the Pastor of our church, Rev. Stanford L. Vinson would have the congregation recite this Psalm.

Then as a child I experienced nightmares for a little while. One night I ran to my parents' room and was instructed to recite this Psalm before bed... That was my last nightmare.

As an adult seeking God for help in teaching His people how to hear His voice, He gave me Psalm 100.

Wow! Something in this Psalm 100 clearly highlights the presence of the Lord in one's life and atmosphere. Thank you to my childhood Pastor, I know all the words.

There was something very special about Pastor Vinson... Yes he baptized me; he encouraged continuous education; he believed in financial security and owning properties –securing his children, their children, and the generations to come; he lived by *If God said it, I believe it, and that settles it*; he desired to *Spray everyone with The Holy Ghost*; I obtained his 2 required degrees BA (Born Again) and PWG (Power with God)... Pastor Vinson is also my maternal grandfather.

Rev. Stanford L. Vinson

Papa, this book is dedicated to you.
Thank You.
See you on the other side.

4

Table of Contents

This Devotional requires a Notebook for Journaling.

Day 1 – Speak with Me

God is speaking to me….

How is He speaking?

How can I distinguish God's voice from my own?

Was that you God?

The above are questions are that many of us Christians have.

When I was trying to get closer with God, I would hear people say, *God said... or I was talking with the Lord...* I would just get irritated or be in awe. I wondered why God didn't speak to me like that. I desired to hear Him like I heard a human's voice.

Then I tried another route. Maybe if I can ask God for signs! I wanted to know if the guy I was dating was *the one*. I asked the Lord to make lightning appear in the sky...

One day I was at church and a minister walked up to me and handed me a scripture.

1 Kings 19:11-12
11 And he said, Go forth, and stand upon the mount before the Lord.
And, behold, the Lord passed by, and a great and strong wind rent the mountains,
and brake in pieces the rocks before the Lord; but the Lord was not in the wind:

and after the wind an earthquake; but the Lord was not
in the earthquake:
12 And after the earthquake a fire; but the Lord was not
in the fire:
and after the fire a still small voice.

I was making this too difficult. I was looking for big signs, the Lord to part the sky and come out of a cloud.

Even though God can speak to us in various ways, He was trying to communicate with me in the *still, gentle voice.*

Let us Calm the noise in our life, Be still in God, and Listen.

This devotional will take you on a journey of listening.

JOURNAL
THIS DEVOTIONAL REQUIRES A NOTEBOOK FOR JOURNALING

1. Write down 1Kings 19:12b.

2. List different ways you can have a quiet time with the Lord.

3. When can you have those quiet times this week? Read this devotional and do the journaling during those times (you will need at least 30-60 min each day)

Day 2 – Joyful Noise

Okay Lord... is their some formula to how I can talk to You and hear You?

Every Christian has a personal way they get to the Throne of God. For those of us searching for a way to attain that Presence, we all wonder the same thing. Is there a guideline or example to follow, until we can establish our unique way of communicating with the Father? Psalms 100 gives us an outline.

*Make a **joyful noise unto the Lord**,*
all ye lands (people).
Serve the Lord with gladness:
*come before His **PRESENCE** with **singing***
*Know ye the Lord **He is God:***
*it is **He that hath made us**,*
and not we ourselves;
***we are His people**,*
and the sheep of His pasture.
*Enter into His gates with **thanksgiving**,*
*and into His courts with **praise**:*
*be **thankful unto Him**,*
*and **bless His name**.*
*For **the Lord is good**;*
*His **mercy is everlasting**;*
*and **His truth endureth** to all generations.*

We will put this altogether later; however, today let us practice verse 1 of Psalms 100.

Make a Joyful Noise unto the Lord,
all ye lands (people).

How can you make a joyful noise unto God?

Close your eyes and think about someone you would be happy to see; it could be your spouse, child, parents, sibling, or a friend. Now, how would you greet them? What would you say?

Now, magnify your greeting (Psalms) 100 times... That is your joyful noise!

Some greeting examples: *GOD YOU ARE GREAT! Hallelujah! Hey! MMMMM! GLORY!*

Note: Psalm 22:3 But thou art holy, O thou that inhabitest the praises of Israel.

JOURNAL

1. Write down some noise phrases, some words that God can hear from your lips.

2. For the next 10 minutes just say the phrases and words from number one, clap your hands... Offer them joyfully to the Lord.

3. Now write down what you felt as you made a joyful noise to God.
    Be sure to use every part of your five senses to describe what and how you felt.
    (This is important as we grow in our closeness to God.)
    Did you feel anything on any parts of your body? Did you smell anything specific? See anything? Hear anything? Taste anything?

Day 3 – Serve with Gladness

Let us look at the beginning of Psalm 100:2 today.

Serve the Lord with gladness:
*come before His **PRESENCE** with **singing***

Verse 2a - SERVE THE LORD WITH GLADNESS
Gladness is a noun. The biblical translation is simchah (sim-kha) meaning *joy, mirth, pleasure, glad result, happy issue*

Be happy about being a Christian! All the complaining, bitterness, hatred, jealousy, sadness, depression...keep it off your face and remove all from your thoughts and heart!

You serve the True and Living God, for that reason you should embody the joy of the Lord (which is your strength) and retain a smile on your face. Does God deserve that?

*Note - Be aware of how serving God with gladness
is the preface to His Presence!

JOURNAL

1. Are you serving the Lord with gladness? Consider the meaning of gladness (joy, mirth, pleasure, glad result, happy issue) and write about what that looks like, how would you define it with examples?

2. What do you need to remove from your thoughts, mind, emotions, or your presence to achieve this true gladness?

3. What burdens do you need to give to the Lord to achieve gladness?

4. Write – *The Joy of the Lord is my Strength*
Nehemiah 8:10b - *For this day is holy unto our Lord: neither be ye sorry; for the joy of the Lord is your strength.*

5. How does serving the Lord, gladness, joy and strength go together?

6. Why do you think *Serve the Lord with Gladness* is written prior to *Come before His Presence*?

Day 4 – Presence with Singing

To understand how God communicates with you, first spend time in His Presence. This requires alone time with just you and God, so you are close enough to hear and feel Him. Being that close to God creates an atmosphere that has no space for distractions, uncertainties, nor questions if what you are experiencing is really Him.

Can you have a *face to face* conversation with someone if they are not in the room with you? No, that is ridiculous! You wouldn't be able to hear them.

How can we expect to hear God if we are not *face to face*, in front of Him... in His Presence?

Let us explore the latter part of Psalm 100:2.
> *Come before His **PRESENCE** with **singing***

Come Before His Presence with Singing

Singing translates biblically in this verse as a *ringing cry, shout for joy, triumphing, or singing.*

Sing a song, listen to a song, or read a Psalm. Is that not simple enough?

It is time for the journaling (on the next page). Read over all 5 steps of the Journal Activity today and then complete it.

JOURNAL

1. Get in a quiet place, where no distractions can happen.

2. Play a song that is triumphant and praises and honors God.

3. Repeat the song... Sing along, move your body to how you feel with the song (clap, fist bump, spin around... whatever comes over you, do it).

4. Settle in the Glory of God and begin to speak and do your own praise for as long as you desire.

5. Write down what you feel, see, hear, smell, and taste while you are in the presence of God.

Day 5 – Humility, Thanksgiving, Mercy and Truth

How Awesome Is Our God!
How Mighty Is Our God!

Let us put together the rest of Psalms 100, as we seek the presence of the one and true Living God!

> Know ye the Lord **He is God**: it is **He that hath made us**, and not we ourselves; **we are His people**, and the sheep of His pasture.
> Enter into His gates with **thanksgiving**, and into His courts with **praise**: be **thankful unto Him**, and **bless His name**.
> For **the Lord is good**; His **mercy is everlasting**; and **His truth endureth** to all generations.

As you come before God, be cognizant of these things:

1. Be Humble
Please note when you are in the presence of the Lord, this is such an awesome experience to behold our Creator...**He is God**, **The One who made us**... You had no parts creating yourself!

2. Have Thanksgiving and Praise All About You
The verse tells us to *enter into His gates with thanksgiving and enter into His courts with praise*. Then the word says be thankful unto Him and Bless His Name.

Did God just repeat Himself?

No – Our state of mind is thanksgiving and praise and then we declare our thankfulness and bless His name.

Have you ever said thank you but didn't really mean it? God wants you to be real and sincere.

3. The Lord Is Good His Mercy Is Everlasting and His Truth Endureth

When you express thanksgiving and praise verbally, blessing the name of Jesus, Recognize The Power!

When you say the name Jesus the Word tells us everything in earth, above earth, and below earth has to succumb! That's why we bind things, break things, release things, claim things, touch things, and pray for things in the name of Jesus.

So bless the Wonderful Name, the Almighty Name, and the Matchless Name of Jesus! Whew, isn't He Good; He will continue to show mercy – compassion, kindness, and forgiveness to little ole you; and His Truth – reality, quality, honesty, loyalty, accuracy, law, word – is forever... You are in the Presence of that!

JOURNAL

1. What does humility look like to you?

2. What are you thankful for? Write 50 things.

3. Write 25 words or phrases of how to bless His name.
   (Bless = salute, praise, adore, cause to kneel)

4. How can you live in a continuous mentality of thanksgiving?

5. How does knowing God's mercy is everlasting make you feel?

6. What does *His Truth Endureth* mean to you?

Day 6 – Put it Together

Put all of Psalms 100 together!

1. Make a Joyful Noise unto the Lord

2. Serve the Lord with Gladness

3. Come Before His Presence with Singing

4. Be Humble – He made us

5. Have Thanksgiving and Praise all about You

6. The Lord is Good, His Mercy Everlasting, and His Truth Endureth to all Generations

Now, go to a quiet place where there are not any distractions. <u>Read over the following 8 steps and the Journal first,</u> for understanding of what should happen, and then complete them.

1. Begin with Joyful Noise unto God – (Hallelujah, claps... spend at least 5 minutes on this)

2. Be Happy about coming to your God

3. Read Psalms 24

4. Play some good praise and worship music

5. Thank Him for things He has done

6. Bless Him for who He is to you

7. Just Glorify the Father

8. Sit or lay prostrate (lying stretched out on the ground with one's face downward) in His Presence.

JOURNAL

1. Write down everything your body experienced as you Pray and Praised and Honored and Worshipped God

2. What did you feel in your body, in the atmosphere, see, hear, taste, and/or smell?

With your continuous revisits to His Throne Room, you are creating an atmosphere for God to speak to you. You are ultimately familiarizing yourself with God's voice. Consequently, you will be able to recognize the language of God and how He communicates with you throughout your day.

Day 7 – Take it up a Notch!

Today we will do the Journal first. Then we will plan for a visit with the Lord. Finally, we will conclude with another Journal.

Journal

Write down the Alphabet vertically on your paper, one letter per line. Then write an *Attribute of God* for each letter. (An example is below; make it personal.)

A – Amazing, Adonai...

B – Beautiful

C - Comforter

D – Dew in the Morning

E – Everlasting

F – Friend

G – Great

H – Holy

I – Incredible

J – Jehovah Jireh...

Visit with The Lord

Now, let's begin by going to a quiet place. Take a deep breath, and relax. Sing a song - you can make up a worship song, read a Psalms (Psalms 24 is a good one), and/or have soft worship music playing throughout this experience.

Open the conversation with God. Try the following technique: (take your time, relax in Him, and make it personal)

Tell God who He is –

Lord you are an awesome Creator.

(Use one *Attribute of God* from your alphabet to describe Him.)

Tell Him why He is an awesome Creator –

When I look at the moon and the stars and the flowers and the trees, and all you have created

(Attribute used in the previous step; give a reason why it's true.)

Ask for forgiveness –

Lord forgive me of any wrong I have committed against You or Your creation. Create in me a clean heart and renew Your Spirit in me.

Again tell Him He is a Great God and thank Him for things He has done for you. (Use your thank-you list of 5o from Day 5 Journal.)

Then Bless Him for just who He is –

You are Great, Wonderful, a Healer, Provider, Creator of the Universe, King of Kings, Lord of Lords, Majestic, Omnipresent, Sovereign...

(Go through *Alphabet of Attributes of God*, today's Journal.)

Love and Exalt Him

Lord I love You! God I adore You! I exalt You in this place!

(Use some of your 25 phrases from Day 5 Journal, number 3.)

Give God permission to dwell and abide forever

God please inhabit my space; allow me to experience You, Your throne room, Your Presence, Oh Father - The Holy One.

(Then enter boldly into His Presence, knowing because Jesus died and rose that you might go beyond the veil!)

Holy Spirit dwell and forever abide with me, in my space.

Now, ask God to speak to you...
Be still and listen. Be aware of all your senses.

JOURNAL

1. What happened?

2. Did you experience anything with your 5 senses? (eyes, ears, nose, mouth, touch/feeling)

3. Did you feel tingling? If so, then where did you feel the tingles?

4. Did you hear/feel any words? ...

Day 8 - Again!

This experience of learning how God personally speaks to you, I know it has been amazing. All your journal entries should be full of sensory details of being in the presence of God and hearing His voice.

Here are some examples of people in the faith with us:

- For one person, when God speaks their left eyebrow twitches. Therefore, when He speaks throughout the day and that twitch happens, they know it is God.
- Another may feel the covering of our Lord's love when they smell flowers. (This could lead to a gift in hospitality, intercession, giving, or even exhortation. This person may walk in the room and know who needs to feel God's love because God may highlight the scent when they are next to the person in need.)
- Someone experiences tingling in their right hand when the presence and power of God is on them. (this could be the beginning to the gift of healing)

The goal is to become familiar with what happens to you in His Presence! When God does communicate with you throughout the day, you have no doubt it is Him.

Now let's do it again! Make it more personal! Go to a quiet place. Take a deep breath, and relax. Sing a song, read a Psalms, and/or have soft worship music playing throughout this experience. (When you get finished, *ask God to speak to you* and **Journal** your experience).

Do the following format again:

Tel Tell God who He is –

> *Lord you are an awesome Creator.*
>
> (Use one *Attribute of God* from your alphabet to describe Him.)

Tell Him why He is an Awesome Creator –

> *When I look at the moon and the stars and the flowers and the trees, and all you have created*
>
> (The attribute used in the previous step; give a reason why it's true.)

Ask for forgiveness –

> *Lord forgive me of any wrong I have committed against You or Your creation. Create in me a clean heart and renew Your Spirit in me.*

Again tell Him He is a Great God and thank Him for things He has done for you. (Use some thank yous from your list of 5o in Day 5, entry 2)

Then Bless Him for just who He is –

> *You are Great, Wonderful, a Healer, Provider, Creator of the Universe, King of Kings, Lord of Lords, Majestic, Omnipresent, Sovereign...*
>
> (Go through the alphabet using a word to describe Him for each letter, Day 7)

Love and Exalt Him

> *Lord I love You! God I adore You! I exalt You in this place!*
>
> (Use some of your 25 phrases from Day 5, entry 3)

Give God permission to dwell and abide forever –

> *God please inhabit my space; allow me to experience You, Your throne room, Your Presence, Oh Father - The Holy One.*
>
> (Then enter boldly into His Presence, knowing because Jesus died and rose that you might go beyond the veil!)
>
> *Holy Spirit dwell and forever abide with me, in my space.*

Reminder
Now, ask God to speak to you.
Be still and listen. Be aware of all your senses.
JOURNAL YOUR EXPERIENCE.

Day 9 – Over and Over

Today you will enter the presence of God again.

Reread your journal entries.

Journal 1
Now take a few minutes to write a conclusion of this journey.

Yes, our ultimate goal is to worship The Lord; however, we also desire to hear Him and know Him.

It is so important that you continue to have time with God, just you and Him. This Christian walk is a growth walk. You will continue to learn the ways the Lord speaks to you and develop in those ways as He cultivates your spiritual gifts.

Keep on spending time with The Lord over and over again! This quality time is spent in Prayer, Praise, and Worship - Getting in His PRESENCE!

Be mindful of the outline of Psalms 100: an aura of complete humility and thankfulness, remembering His goodness, recalling His mercy, and knowing His truth is forever.

Now go before the Lord. Be cognizant of the following:

> *Take your time through each step. Be sincere.
> It will flow naturally.

*You may be so overwhelmed by His presence, you might find yourself snorting and crying. You may feel so much power that you want to lay down. Go with whatever you're feeling, and do not fight it... The Spirit is moving in, through and around you.

*Know everyone's experience is not the same. You may hear His voice differently than someone else. You may even spend more time in one of the areas (suggested steps) than another. It is all okay; do what feels natural to your spirit.

*You may also come up with your own formula to abide in His Presence, Great! The outline given in this devotional was just to get you started.

*Continue revisiting His Throne daily (at the least). Pay close attention to what God's communication feels like and sounds like; maybe even how it smells, taste, or looks like. You will become comfortable when God speaks because you have experienced His presence. Hence when God speaks to you throughout your day, you'll know it is Him.

*After you complete your private time in His Presence, **JOURNAL!** If The Spirit leads you to write something down, **JOURNAL!** *Be careful not to get so caught up in writing or journaling so much during your private time in His presence. Why? Sometimes we, all people in general, can get so caught up in a task that we miss the moment. So sparingly write throughout or wait until the end. DO NOT MISS THE MOMENT. **Just be led by The Spirit**.*

*Notice how God speaks to you throughout the day. What is He doing to communicate with you? Pay attention to your senses. **JOURNAL** what happens and new things that occur in you and with God's voice to you.

*A few reasons why it is important to JOURNAL:
- You will be able to read how you experience God and how He develops His presence in you.
- You will notice different things happen to you when God wants to inform you of something or require you to do something.
- Journal entries will show your development in a certain area or use of a spiritual gift. Be sure to date every entry.

Time to seek out His Presence again!

You may use the formula outlined on Day 7 and Day 8, variations of that formula, or our own. Remember your *Alphabet Attributes of God*, *Thank You List*, and your *25 Ways to Bless The Lord*.

Now, get in your quiet space and begin.

Conclusion

Keep the lines of communication open all day.

You say something, God communicates back -that is prayer continuously!

Follow *The Commandment* - love God and love your neighbor as God loves you. If we handled life and people as God loves, WOW!

Make sure you are ALWAYS IN A POSITION TO HEAR GOD; therefore, WALK IN LOVE AND ACT IN LOVE.

GOD IS LOVE, Stay Connected.

[28] Then one of the scribes came, and having heard them reasoning together, perceiving that He had answered them well, asked Him, "Which is the first commandment of all?" [29] Jesus answered him, "The first of all the commandments *is:* 'Hear, O Israel, the Lord our God, the Lord is one. [30] **And you shall love the Lord your God with all your heart, with all your soul, with all your mind, and with all your strength.'** This *is* the first commandment. [31] And the second, like *it,* is this: 'You shall love your neighbor as yourself.' There is no other commandment greater than these." [32] So the scribe said to Him, "Well *said,* Teacher. You have spoken the truth, for there is one God, and there is no other but He. [33] And to love Him with all the heart, with all the understanding, with all the soul, and with all the strength, and to love one's neighbor as oneself, is more than all the whole burnt offerings and sacrifices." [34] Now when Jesus saw that he answered wisely, He said to him, "You are not far from the kingdom of God." – Mark 12:28-34 NKJV

MoWorshipMoGospel – 2009, 2019

www.moworshipmogospel.com

HE IS COMING BACK

May Your Conversation and Behavior... Your Life

Be Lived in Such a Way that Anticipates

THE ARRIVAL OF KING OF KINGS

Made in the USA
Columbia, SC
08 June 2020